T1 P ond *of a*

by Steven Tucker
illustrated by Graham Smith

Harcourt
SCHOOL PUBLISHERS

Printed in China

ISBN 10: 0-15-351506-6
ISBN 13: 978-0-15-351506-4

Ordering Options
ISBN 10: 0-15-351213-X (Grade 3 Advanced Collection)
ISBN 13: 978-0-15-351213-1 (Grade 3 Advanced Collection)
ISBN 10: 0-15-358096-8 (package of 5)
ISBN 13: 978-0-15-358096-3 (package of 5)

4 5 6 7 8 9 10 0940 12 11 10 09

At first glance, a small pond may not seem like a very busy place. A duck drifts gently across the surface. A bee buzzes past. A frog sends his song across the water. Cattails nod in the breeze. The pond appears to be peaceful and calm.

A pond is actually filled with activity! From the water's edge to the muddy bottom, millions of living things make their homes in and around even the smallest pond.

Each of these creatures is busy searching for food and trying to survive. All seek shelters to protect them from creatures that may want to eat them. They hide from predators and protect their young.

Different creatures live in different parts of a pond. The dim water at the bottom is very different from the bright surface at the top.

An old pond has different conditions from a new one. Some ponds are there permanently, and some will disappear in a short time. Some come and go.

To think about life in a pond, ask some questions. Take that duck, paddling across the water. What does it eat? Perhaps it eats small fish. What do those fish eat? Perhaps they eat insects. What do the insects eat? Perhaps they eat grasses and weeds. How do those grasses grow?

The answers show how living things make up an ecosystem. An ecosystem is a community of plants and animals in one place. An ecosystem could be as small as a glass of water or as large as the entire earth.

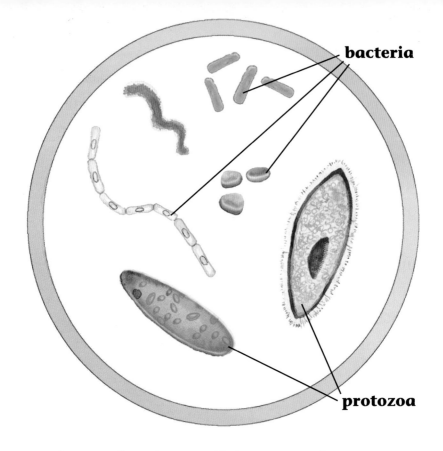

The smallest forms of life in a pond are
bacteria. They may be shaped like dots or
small rods. Most are too small to see without
a microscope. Larger life forms called protozoa
feed on bacteria. Some protozoa have legs that
whip around to help them move, and some
simply float. The largest protozoa may be only
four millimeters long. That's about the size of
two or three small letters in a newspaper!

Other tiny plants and animals also live in ponds. Some are tiny worms, some resemble small flowers, and others look like plants. They eat bacteria, too. They also eat each other, and larger animals feed upon them.

Algae are simple living things that form the green scum on ponds. Billions of them can take over a pond. They use up the oxygen in a pond, and when oxygen becomes scarce, other life forms disappear.

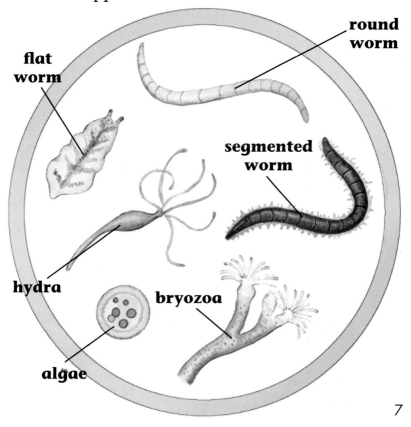

round worm

flat worm

segmented worm

hydra

bryozoa

algae

Arthropods also live on ponds. These include mites, spiders, crayfish-like animals, and insects. There are thousands of types of arthropods, and most are tiny. Fairy shrimp and water lice are about the size of a pencil eraser. Crayfish are larger and may be a few inches long. Spiders are usually small, but some pond spiders may grow to four inches (10.1cm) across. Most arthropods prey on smaller creatures and even each other. They have legs or tails to move, and mouths and claws to grasp their victims. All around the pond, fierce battles go on all the time.

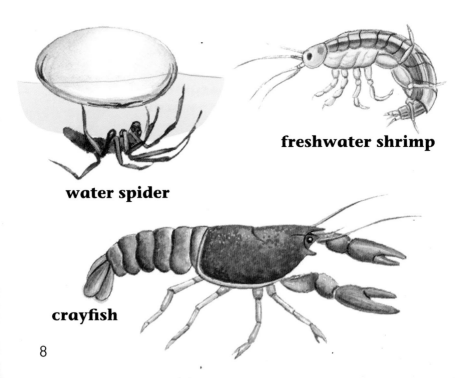

freshwater shrimp

water spider

crayfish

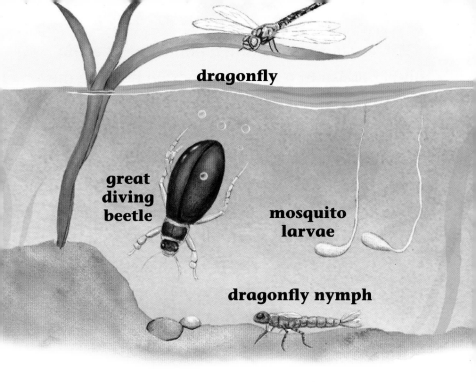

dragonfly

great diving beetle

mosquito larvae

dragonfly nymph

An amazing variety of insects live in ponds. Some live their whole lives under the water. Other insects, such as dragonflies, live their lives in stages. When they are young, dragonflies live under the water and are called nymphs. After a time, they crawl up from the water, and their bodies change. Then they take to the air.

Water beetles have tough shells to protect them. They have strong jaws, and they are fierce hunters. Even the toughest insect, though, may be a meal for a larger animal.

Fish eat many insects in a pond. The size and number of fish in a pond depends on how big the pond is and what else lives there.

Different types of fish live in different places. Catfish and carp root around in the muddy bottom for food. Mosquito fish feed near the surface of shallow waters. Shiners hide in weeds. Sunfish and bluegills swim all over the pond but like places with weeds where they feel safe. Bass are usually the largest fish in ponds. How big they get depends on how much food is available.

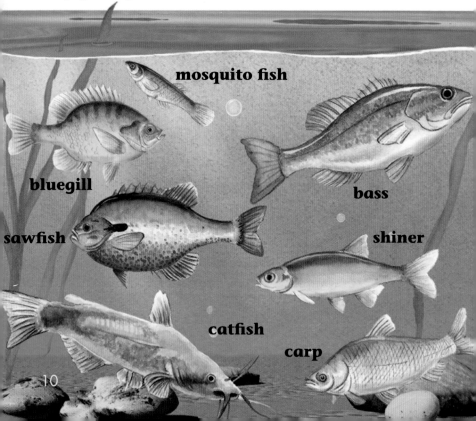

mosquito fish

bluegill

bass

sawfish

shiner

catfish

carp

Turtles and snakes live in ponds. Although many people fear snakes, few water snakes are harmful. Salamanders also live in or near ponds. They move quickly and are difficult to spot.

Reptiles that live in ponds live part of their lives away from the water. Reptiles lay their eggs on land. Sometimes their eggs and young become food for other animals near the pond.

Can you imagine a pond without frogs? First, the frogs lay their eggs in the water, and the eggs become tadpoles. Tadpoles are born with gills like a fish. The gills grow closed, and the tadpole begins to breathe air. The tadpoles then grow leg buds and lose their tails. After just a few weeks, a tadpole becomes a frog.

Frogs are both predators and prey. Adult frogs can eat small fish and even mice. Snakes, turtles, otters, raccoons, and birds may hunt frogs.

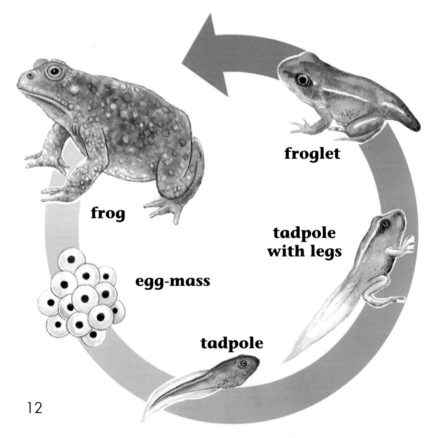

froglet

frog

tadpole
with legs

egg-mass

tadpole

Many kinds of birds may live near ponds. Otters, raccoons, skunks, foxes, and coyotes are also drawn to the pond to find water and food.

All animals depend on others. Large animals feed on smaller ones. Smaller animals feed on still smaller ones. This cycle is called a food chain. It is really more of a pyramid. There are many creatures at the base. Fewer animals are at the top. The larger the animal, the more food it needs.

Ponds have a life cycle, too. Over time, rain washes things into the pond. It slowly fills up. Over a long time, it may turn into a marsh. One day the pond will completely disappear.

The absence of life in a pond may mean trouble. Harmful chemicals may have washed into it. Maybe weeds have taken it over. Maybe one type of animal has wiped out all others.

Some people work to keep ponds healthy. These people manage the plants and animals. They may add or take out fish. They think carefully about the ecosystem. A pond is a little world. The world is a big ecosystem.

Think Critically

1. What is an ecosystem?

2. How might you tell an old pond from a young one?

3. Describe what happens first when a tadpole becomes a frog. What happens next? What happens last?

4. What happens when algae take over a pond?

5. Which creatures do you think would disappear first as a pond begins to fill in? Why?

 Science

Compare Ecosystems A pond is an ecosystem. Think of other places that could be ecosystems. Choose one of them and list the living things that exist there. Then think about the food chain of the ecosystem. Which of the things on your list would be at the top of the food chain and which would be on the bottom?

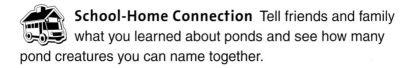 **School-Home Connection** Tell friends and family what you learned about ponds and see how many pond creatures you can name together.

Word Count: 1,023(1,063)